D0908850

THE GREAT OUTDOORS!

Snow Sports

MC

Mason Crest

THE GREAT OUTDOORS!

Camping

Discovering Nature

Fishing

Hiking and Backpacking

Horseback Riding

Hunting

Mountain Biking

Snow Sports

Survival Skills

Water Sports

Snow Sports

DIANE BAILEY

Mason Crest
450 Parkway Drive, Suite D
Broomall, PA 19008
www.masoncrest.com

Printed and bound in the United States of America.

Series ISBN: 978-1-4222-3565-2
Hardback ISBN: 978-1-4222-3573-7
EBook ISBN: 978-1-4222-8318-9

First printing
1 3 5 7 9 8 6 4 2

Produced by Shoreline Publishing Group LLC
Santa Barbara, California
Editorial Director: James Buckley Jr.
Designer: Patty Kelley
Production: Sandy Gordon
www.shorelinepublishing.com

Cover photographs by Monkey Business Images/Dreamstime.com.

Names: Bailey, Diane, 1966- author.
Title: Snow sports / by Diane Bailey.
Description: Broomall, PA : Mason Crest, 2017. | Series: The Great Outdoors |
    Includes webography and index.
Identifiers: LCCN 2016002453| ISBN 9781422235737 (Hardback) | ISBN
    9781422235652 (Series) | ISBN 9781422283189 (EBook)
Subjects: LCSH: Winter sports--Juvenile literature.
Classification: LCC GV841.15 .M35 2017 | DDC 796.9--dc23
LC record available at http://lccn.loc.gov/2016002453

CONTENTS

KEY ICONS TO LOOK FOR

 Words to Understand: These words with their easy-to-understand definitions will increase the reader's understanding of the text, while building vocabulary skills.

 Sidebars: This boxed material within the main text allows readers to build knowledge, gain insights, explore possibilities, and broaden their perspectives by weaving together additional information to provide realistic and holistic perspectives.

 Research Projects: Readers are pointed toward areas of further inquiry connected to each chapter. Suggestions are provided for projects that encourage deeper research and analysis.

 Text-Dependent Questions: These questions send the reader back to the text for more careful attention to the evidence presented here.

 Series Glossary of Key Terms: This back-of-the-book glossary contains terminology used throughout this series. Words found here increase the reader's ability to read and comprehend higher-level books and articles in this field.

 Educational Videos: Readers can view videos by scanning our QR codes, providing them with additional educational content to supplement the text. Examples include news coverage, moments in history, speeches, iconic sports moments and much more!

WORDS TO UNDERSTAND

black diamond a sign in this shape shows the most difficult and dangerous type of ski run

carve a fast, precise turn that uses the edges of skis or snowboards

complement to naturally go with something else

Zamboni a motorized vehicle that smooths ice in rinks by melting it and letting it refreeze

CHAPTER 1

Into the Great Outdoors!

When the weather forecast calls for a snow-storm, a lot of people want to huddle up by the fire with a cup of hot chocolate. Sure, it can be fun to get snowed in. But it's even more fun to get snowed out! It's easy enough to build a snowman in the yard, or you could get a snowball fight going. But maybe you run out of carrots for noses. Or maybe you get sore arms from throwing (or being hit). Then it's time to venture into new territory.

If you are not used to winter sports, you may find they take a little more effort to do. But the payoff is worth it. It's exhilarating to shred a mountainside of fresh powder on skis or a snow-board, master a figure eight on ice skates, or trek through a fresh snowfall in the woods. One of the best parts of conquering the snow and ice is that it takes a whole different set of skills than other sports. So get ready for a challenge!

Whether you like skiing, snowboarding, ice skating or snowshoeing, there are plenty of choices. You don't have to stay inside and let the weather win. And there's always hot chocolate waiting at the end.

History of Snow Sports

When mother nature dumps three feet of snow on the ground, life may slow down for a little while. But it can't stop forever! Skiing, ice skating, and other winter sports started as important ways to travel through the snow and ice when regular shoes were not enough.

Northern people have been using skis for centuries, in peace and war.

WINTER WARFARE

Winter Warfare

In wartime, soldiers cannot wait until the weather clears up. Historically, wars that happened in the winter meant soldiers had to find a way to fight even in snow and ice. Records show many battles that were fought on skis, perhaps as early as the 12th century. Army forces from Russia, Finland, Italy, Norway, and the United States have all been trained in ski combat. Troops in the Netherlands carried ice skates along with their rifles. They were able to move on the frozen water much more quickly than their enemies, giving them the advantage of speed.

Skiing is probably the oldest of the winter sports. Archaeologists have found wooden skis from more than 5,000 years ago. Places like Russia, Finland, and Norway got a lot of snow—and it stuck around for months. Skis were a necessary form of transportation. These ancient peoples were cross-country skiing. They used the skis to slide easily on the surface of the snow. Downhill skiing began around the mid-1800s. It is also called Alpine skiing because it became popular in the Alps, a mountain range in Europe. By this time, skiing was not just a way to get around. People did it just for fun—and nothing was more fun than racing down a mountainside at top speed.

Snowshoes are another ancient form of transportation. People attached wide, flat platforms onto their feet. There was more surface area touching the ground, so it spread out the weight of their bodies. This kept them from sinking down in the snow. Ice skating also dates back several thousand years. At first, people tied animal bones to their feet and simply slid across the ice. Later they used a metal blade that cut into the ice. A lot of sports and activities have come from ice skating. Some people like to do fancy moves in figure skating, while others go as fast as they can on speed skates. Hockey is another popular sport played on skates.

Snowboarding has become very popular with younger snow lovers.

By the middle of the 20th century, there was a newcomer to snow sports. Snowboarding put the thrills of downhill skiing onto a single board. It is similar to a surfboard or skateboard. Young people especially took to snowboarding. At first, many skiers did not like snowboarding. Some of them thought that the "one-plankers" did not respect the traditions of skiing. Snowboards carved the snow differently, and made it more difficult for skiers who followed them on the slopes. Snowboarding was not just a short-lived fad, though. By the 1990s it was getting so popular that ski resorts started allowing snowboarders in. Although some rivalry still exists between the two sports, it's more friendly now. Lots of skiers decided to give snowboarding a try and found they liked it.

Snow Sports Heat Up

Not surprisingly, snow sports are more popular in areas that have long winters and get lots of snow. You will find more skiers in Colorado and Canada than in Florida! However, with new technology, it does not have to be winter to enjoy winter sports. Pump in some electricity, and indoor ice rinks can be kept frozen all year long. When the ice gets messy, **Zambonis** roll over to create a new, fresh sheet of ice.

Figure skating combines athleticism, grace, and balletic movement.

A huge boost to winter sports was the invention of artificial snow. (It's still real snow, but the process of making it is artificial.) In 1950, three men in Connecticut experimented with making artificial snow by spraying water through a garden hose into the cold air. It froze into snow. It took a couple of decades for artificial snow to catch on, but now many ski resorts make snow when the weather does not cooperate.

What's the most popular winter sport? Alpine skiing is the most popular in the United States, with almost 9.4 million people taking part. Next up comes snowboarding, with about 7.7 million people hitting the slopes. Snowshoeing is also quickly growing in popularity. Of course, lots of people do more than one sport—and sometimes they do not even wait for the cold months!

 ## TAKE A LESSON

It's true: learning isn't as much fun as doing. The idea of taking lessons can seem like a waste of time. In the long run, though, learning from someone who knows what they are doing can *save* you a lot of time—and probably a few falls. Lessons are especially important in skiing and snowboarding.

It's easy to get hurt when you're hurtling down a mountain. Some skills may feel strange at first. Your body might not want to naturally do what it should. Instead, you'll need to learn and then practice these skills until they become second nature. Most ski resorts have professionals on hand who can show you a few basics before you hit the slopes.

Cross-country skiing is one of the best overall workouts you can get.

Choosing Your Sport

The type of winter sport that you choose will probably depend on where you live. Unless you live in the mountains, you will have to travel to a resort to get in some downhill time on skis or a snowboard. Other activities, such as cross-country skiing or snowshoeing, can be done in a lot of places, as long as there's snow! If skating is your thing, many places have ice skating rinks. If not, you can try a frozen pond or lake. (Be sure the ice is frozen thick!)

Like most outdoor activities, skiing is best enjoyed with others.

You may choose a sport that **complement**s activities you do in warmer weather. Runners might like the idea of long-distance cross-country treks through the snow, for example. That will help them keep in shape during the off-season. If you have experience with surfing, water skiing, or skateboarding, then skiing and snowboarding are natural crossovers.

Winter sports are great for getting a good aerobic workout. In addition, they work your leg muscles and core strength. Even if you play other sports during the year, you may find that your winter workout is even more strenuous!

Some winter sports, such as hockey, are played in teams. However, most of them are geared to individual participation. You can learn at your own pace, and it's up to you to decide when to try a new ice skating jump, a gnarly **carve** on a snowboard, or a run down a treacherous **black diamond** slope. Even if you aren't on a team, outdoor winter sports should never be done alone. There are risks in being out in the cold and off the beaten path. Don't tackle the slopes or the countryside without a buddy, in case you get in trouble.

 ## TEXT-DEPENDENT QUESTIONS

1. What material was used in the first ice skates?

2. How do snowshoes work?

3. What is the most popular winter sport in the United States?

 ## RESEARCH PROJECT

Skiing has a history that goes back thousands of years. Look up some of the major milestones about how the sport and its equipment have developed over the years.

Snow Sports History

 WORDS TO UNDERSTAND

crampon a spike that attaches to shoes to improve traction

friction the resistance that happens when two surfaces rub together

mogul a bump on a ski slope that is formed after many skiers have pushed the snow together

parallel two objects that are side-by-side and have an equal amount of distance between them

piste a marked, prepared trail for skiing

traction the grip or contact that an object has with another surface

CHAPTER 2

Getting It Done Right

ou don't swim in a rip current. You don't take a bike ride during an ice storm. You don't send a little guy out to guard the big man. When you want to get good results—and stay safe—you have to use a little common sense. That's especially true in snow sports, where the weather and conditions can be especially challenging. It's important to be aware of your surroundings and know your limits.

Check it Out

n snow sports, the first thing to know is that snow is not *just* snow. It may be powdery or packed, wet or dry, fresh or choppy. Experienced skiers and snowboarders

A well-groomed "piste" offers smooth skiing for everyone.

check out conditions in advance. They learn how to read the snow, so they know what skills or equipment they might need to use.

Beginners should start on groomed ski runs called **pistes**. They are prepared and maintained by the employees at a ski resort. They have marked trails for people to follow. Pistes are often monitored by a ski patrol that looks for people who have gotten into trouble. These runs are usually the safest. Off-piste trails are off the beaten track. These are not maintained and are less predictable.

In a way, skiing, snowboarding, or snowshoeing is like taking a trip. Whether it's down a hill or across the countryside, you're going from Point A to Point B. It's a good idea to plan your "trip" in advance. You could be navigating through stands of trees, or over bumps of snow called **moguls**. It's important to first "find the line." That means figuring out how you're going to make your way down a hill or through a course. That way, you cut down on your chances of getting stuck or having an accident.

One risk in skiing is avalanches. These aren't a big problem at most ski resorts, but they can be a problem on high mountains, backcountry trails, and in fresh snowfalls. If you will be skiing or boarding in a dangerous area, always check conditions beforehand, go with a buddy, and carry appropriate safety gear.

You don't want to be below this thundering avalanche of snow.

Ice skating holds different risks. Rinks are safe, but ponds and lakes can be dangerous if the ice is too thin. Make sure the ice is at least a few inches thick, and stay away from water that is newly frozen. The temperature should be below freezing for several days in a row to make sure the ice is hard and thick. Avoid ice that is cracked or has holes, or places where the ice is mixed with running water.

On the Slopes

There may be some rivalry between skiers and snowboarders, but they also have a lot in common. Many of the skills needed to master the slopes cross over between the two sports. Good balance and making both smooth and sharp turns are critical for shredders of both kinds. So is knowing how to stop!

Unless you are a born natural, there's no easy path to the top—or the bottom—of a mountain. For beginners, even standing up on skis can be tricky. Snowboards tend to slide out from under you. You won't get anywhere if you can't stand up, though, so the first thing to master is balance.

The width of your stance is one factor that affects balance. Some skiers like to take a wider stance. This makes them more stable. They can use each foot more independently. A narrower stance is often good for making sharper, more agile turns, however. The big decision a snowboarder must make about stance is which foot to put forward. Most snowboarders ride with their left foot in front, but some ride "goofy," meaning they put their right foot forward. To find out which one you are, have someone give you a gentle push from the back. Do you step forward with your left or right foot to get your balance? That's probably the foot you'll put in the front of a snowboard.

Now it's time to get moving. In downhill skiing or snowboarding, gravity will take care of a lot of that. Part of your job is to make sure it doesn't take you where you *don't* want to go. For that, you'll need to master turning. A common turn in skiing is the **parallel** turn. Skiers line up their skis so they are spaced evenly apart. Then they bend their knees in the same direction they want to turn. The skis will turn so that they are angled across the slope, not pointing straight down it. During the turn, skiers put most of their body weight on the downhill ski (the one farthest down the slope). They zig-zag down the hill by bending their knees and leaning into the turn, shifting their weight and skis back and forth. Snowboarding turns work a similar way, but of course, there is only one board to turn. A boarder leads into a turn by turning his head and shoulders in that direction, then shifts the weight of his feet and body to move the board.

Experienced skiers and snowboarders often do carving turns. They use the edges of their skis or boards to create a line through the snow. This type of turn is harder to master, but it causes less **friction** between

Advanced skiers can turn by leaning so that one edge of their skis bites into the snow.

Snowboarding calls for balance and body control.

the snow and the skis or board. It's possible to keep higher speeds during this turn.

There are many variations on turning, but they all come down to mastering balance and body movements. Falling down is part of the process, but fortunately, it does not take too long to get comfortable with some basic moves and skills. Once you can maneuver with confidence, you can add in speed and more difficult moves.

Making Tracks

 n cross-country skiing and snowshoeing, instead of going down, you're going across the terrain. It's like a very snowy hike, but with better footwear!

Cross-country skiing can be done two ways: classic and skate. In classic, skiers simply push their skis forward in a straight line. In skate style, they push their skis at a V-shaped angle, like in ice skating. Skate style allows skiers to go faster, but it requires more energy and skill.

The basic technique in cross-country skiing is called the shuffle. Skiers don't lift their feet; they just slide them forward, using poles to help them push off. Shuffling is a pretty easy skill to acquire. Most people can pick it up in a few minutes. Once you get comfortable with that, you can focus on leaning forward slightly and transferring more of your body weight to the front. This will give you more power to plow through the snow. (The boots you wear let your heels come off the ski to help give you power.)

Gravity only works one way in downhill skiing, but cross-country skiers must learn to manage it in two directions. On a downhill, they need to control their speed. The snowplow is a technique where skiers point the tips of the skis together. They form an arrow shape. This causes friction between the ski and the snow and helps slow the skier down.

For the challenge of getting uphill, skiers use the herringbone. This is like a reverse of the snowplow. The tips of the skis point outward, in a V-shape. The inside edges of the skis are angled down, into the snow. This gives skiers enough **traction** to overcome the natural tendency to slip backward. Then they can walk uphill.

Another technique is moving sideways along the face of a mountain. This may be necessary if the terrain is particularly rough, or if there are obstacles in the way. Push the uphill side of your skis into the snow, and shift your weight to that side.

Snowshoeing doesn't have the glamour or speed of skiing and snowboarding, but it's much simpler to do. It's also a great workout! It's no wonder snowshoeing is one of the fastest-growing winter sports in the world. Snowshoeing is basically walking in the snow. The special, wide shoes have a lot of surface area to keep you "floating" on the surface. Loose snow is the best for snowshoeing. It gives the shoes something to dig into. Snowshoes will slide around on hard snow or icy surfaces.

Walking on a flat surface is pretty straightforward, but of course, the countryside is not always flat. A good technique for going uphill is the kick-step. As you lift your foot and move it forward, kick into the

With a few lessons, this could be you, too, right? Give it a try!

snow and then stamp down. This builds a shelf of snow to support your weight and gives the **crampons** on the bottom of the shoe something to dig into.

Put it on Ice

ven if there is no snow, you can still enjoy some cold-weather fun with ice skating. Three popular types of ice skating are figure, hockey, and speedskating.

Figure skaters are known for doing elaborate spins and jumps. Speedskaters zoom around a rink at speeds that can reach more than 30 miles (48 km) per hour. Hockey requires its own skating skills, combined with game strategies. Of course, hockey players also get to skate with a stick, which they can use to help them balance and turn.

Most people learn to skate on either figure or hockey skates. Some people think one kind is easier to learn; some people will say the other kind. The bottom line is, it probably doesn't matter. Just pick the style you think you want to do, and get started. You can always switch if you want.

It may be a bit tricky at first to stand up on a pair of skates. After all, it's just a thin blade you have to balance on! In a way, it is similar to riding a bike. It's hard to balance on a bike that is standing still. As you start pedaling, though, it gets easier. You'll probably find that once you get moving on a pair of skates, your natural instincts for balance will help you. (Some rinks now have skating aids that look like personal walkers for injured people. You hold onto a bar about chest height as you skate along the ice. The walker helps you keep your balance while you learn the moves of skating. It might look odd, but it works!)

Speedskaters stay in a low crouch to cut down air resistance.

Basic skating is a cross between walking and skiing. The feet move independently to create strokes, and the slippery nature of the ice helps the skate glide across the ice. Besides the basic stroke forward, skaters also can propel themselves by bending their knees and pushing their legs to transfer power to their skates. They don't even have to lift their feet. This is one way they skate backward.

To make small turns on skates, skaters can lean their bodies and bend their skates in the direction they want to go. For bigger turns, they can use a crossover move. They lift one foot and cross it all the way over the other one. Crossovers can also be done backward.

Ice hockey players use skates with two side-by-side blades on each boot.

Practice, practice, practice. You've heard it before, and there's no getting around it. Along the way, there will probably be some sore muscles and maybe some spectacular wipeouts. But if you take the time to learn some skills properly, you will have fewer falls, faster runs, stronger strokes, and better turns.

Oh, yeah—and more fun.

 ## TEXT-DEPENDENT QUESTIONS

1. What is an advantage to a carving turn?

2. What direction do skis point in a herringbone move?

3. What move do skaters use to make big turns?

 ## RESEARCH PROJECT

One of the best ways to learn new skills is to watch other people doing them. Look up some videos of people demonstrating some basic moves in the sport that interests you the most.

CHAPTER 3

Get Great Gear

ood skills are the foundation of any sport, but the right gear helps you master them. Some snow sports can be expensive, but you don't need to fork over a lot of cash just to start out. Many snow sports take place at ski resorts or ice rinks, where you can rent equipment. That's a good way to try out different types of gear to see what you like. You can find out if you prefer short skis or long ones, or if figure skates or hockey skates are more your style.

 WORDS TO UNDERSTAND

intermediate a skill level in between beginner and expert

sidecut a measurement that is the difference between the width of the ends and the middle of skis or a snowboard

synthetic manmade, often to imitate a natural material

With all the choices available, you'll be able to find skis that fit your needs.

Once you really get into a sport, you may decide to buy your own equipment. That will be cheaper in the long run. It also lets you choose exactly what you want within your budget. Don't worry if you can't afford the best skis or skates on the market. High-end equipment is often aimed at experts. Beginners and intermediate athletes can have just as much fun using more affordable equipment.

Skis and Snowboards

here are many types of skis and snowboards, all designed for different styles on the slopes. Some are built for speed. Others are more maneuverable. Stability is another factor.

Most skis are slightly curved. The ends are a little wider than the waist (the middle). The difference between these two measurements is known as the **sidecut**. A deeper sidecut (more curve) lets the rider make faster, sharper turns. However, for fast speeds, straighter skis are more stable. Another thing to consider is the overall length of the ski. Longer skis are stable but more difficult to maneuver. Many beginners prefer to learn on short skis. They aren't quite as stable, but they are much easier to turn.

BOOTS AND BINDINGS

Boots and bindings are other essential pieces of equipment for skiers and snowboarders. Boots are the way your feet "communicate" with the skis. A stiff boot transfers more power from your body into the ski. These are good for advanced skiers, and they translate to more speed and control on difficult runs. Softer, more flexible boots are usually a little more comfortable, and better for beginners. Bindings connect the boots to the skis and hold the boot in place. They also have release mechanisms that let the boot snap out in case of a nasty fall. That stops the skier's leg from getting twisted around.

Snow conditions also make a difference when choosing a ski. Fresh powder is deep and soft, while snow that's already been heavily skied on may be packed down hard. A ski with a narrow waist measurement is good for hardpacked snow. On the other hand, a wider waist is good on powder. Because there is more surface area touching the snow, skiers are less likely to sink down into the soft snow.

In good snow, a thin, lightweight ski will go the fastest. These are usually best for groomed runs. With off-piste skiing, you can't be sure what you'll get. The snow may have bumps from rocks or logs. It could be cruddy and torn up. Skiers here have to be ready for a variety of conditions. They usually want skis that are fatter, heavier, and generally more sturdy.

There is a lot of overlap between the design of skiing and snowboarding gear. The two main types of snowboards are all-mountain and freestyle. An all-mountain board is a good choice for a beginner. It is versatile and can be taken on both groomed runs and off-piste trails. Freestyle boards are lighter and shorter. They are easy to maneuver, can make sharp turns, and are good for doing tricks. However, they are less stable than a longer board.

It's also possible to get a splitboard. These snowboards are designed for backcountry riding that may include some uphill climbs. The board splits in half the long way, so that it resembles a pair of skis. Riders can then walk uphill when they need to, and then reconnect the board for a ride down.

Snowshoes

Over the mountain and through the woods...and maybe across a log or stream. Snowshoeing can be done in all kinds of places, so choose snowshoes based on the landscape you'll be covering. Some models work best on terrain that is mostly flat. Others are designed to take on some hills or obstacles. Another factor is your weight. Heavier people need a larger shoe with more surface area to distribute their weight. It's also important to consider the condition of

Snowshoes like these use straps to attach to your sturdy winter books.

the snow. Dry, light snow is easy to sink into. Snowshoes with more surface area will work better in that kind of snow. However, keep in mind that larger snowshoes are more difficult to maneuver. For flat areas and snow that is somewhat packed, a simpler shoe will be fine.

Advanced snowshoers can get specialty snowshoes with extra features that help in tough terrain. For steep or icy areas, a snowshoe

Choosing Ice Skates

For proper support, ice skates need to
be laced tightly around each ankle.

with larger crampons will provide more traction. Some snowshoes also come with a "heel lift." This is a small platform on the back of the shoe that flips up. For long or steep hills, this gives the back of your foot a boost and makes the climb a little easier.

Skates

I f you are first learning to skate, you'll probably start off with either figure skates or hockey skates. Either one will work, but each type is different and suited to a certain style of skating. If you know you want to focus on a certain type of skating, then pick those types of skates to learn on. If you're not sure, a figure skate will offer the most support and will be slightly easier to learn on.

The most important difference in the types of skates is in the blade. Even though a figure skate blade is thin, it actually has two sides, with a small hollow down the middle. It makes a slight arch shape. A figure skate also has a jagged edge at the toe called a toe pick. These blades are specially designed for figure skaters to do quick turns and tricks. Figure skates also have a taller boot with more ankle support than a hockey skate.

The blade of a hockey skate also has a slight groove in the middle, but it is not as deep as the one in a figure skate. This makes it easier to turn quickly. The blade does not offer as much control as the one on a figure skate, but that's usually not a problem for hockey players. They are more interested in speed for chasing the puck than in doing elaborate jumps!

Speed skates are another specialized type of skate. They have straight, sharp blades, with no groove in the middle. This causes less friction on the ice, letting the skater go faster. The blades are much longer than those on figure or hockey skates. That also increases speed, but it also makes it more difficult to maneuver. Once you have some experience skating, you may want to try speed skating, but they are not the best kind to learn on.

Goggles are an important piece of equipment for skiers and snowboarders. They cut the glare as the sun reflects off the snow, making it easier to see. They also protect the eyes from sunburn and blowing snow. A regular pair of

goggles is fine, but it's also possible to upgrade to more sophisticated ones. Some goggles have an electronic heads-up display (HUD). The HUD displays information on the inside of the goggles. It provides data such as speed and altitude. There is also a built-in GPS to show location. These high-tech goggles can also record information about the number of runs, or the length of "air time" during a jump.

Dressing for the Cold

With cold-weather sports, one of the most important things to gear up for is the weather itself. It's easy to work up a sweat even in the cold, but if the moisture sticks to your body, you will get chilly in a hurry. Wear clothing that doesn't absorb sweat easily and will stay drier. Avoid cotton, and choose wool or **synthetic** materials instead.

You'll need enough clothing to keep you warm, but you don't want it to be too bulky. Plan to dress in several lighter layers rather than one heavy one. A pair of lightweight waterproof pants is a good idea for the outer layer. You'll also want waterproof gloves, good socks, a hat, and possibly a ski mask that covers most of your face. In extreme cold, your body channels heat to your internal organs. That means your fingers, toes, ears, and nose are the most likely to suffer from frostbite, so make sure you take care of them.

Wear sunscreen if you plan to be outside. Even on cloudy days, snow reflects a lot of sun. This means you can get a sunburn in some weird places—like the insides of your nostrils and even your eyeballs. So, go ahead and poke your fingers up your nose to get sunscreen in there, and wear goggles to protect your eyes.

 TEXT DEPENDENT QUESTIONS

1. How does a splitboard work?

2. What kind of skate has the thinnest blade?

3. What are two reasons to wear goggles when on the slopes?

 RESEARCH PROJECT

You may not be able to buy anything just yet, but you can still go shopping for the equipment you would like to eventually get. Set a budget, decide what features are important to you, and make a list of possibilities for your favorite sport's gear.

Choosing Skis and Snowboards

WORDS TO UNDERSTAND

biathlon a winter sport that combines skiing and target shooting

slalom a type of skiing where skiers or boarders make sharp turns around poles or gates

slopestyle an event where skiers or boarders take on an obstacle course and do jumps and tricks

superpipe an event that involves skiing or boarding inside a large, open tube

CHAPTER 4

Further Adventures

igher. Faster. Longer.

Better.

A lot of sports are about competition, and snow sports are no exception. It's thrilling to watch an expert skier soaring off a jump, or a figure skater spinning at dizzying speeds. Most people like winter sports because they are a good way to get outside during cold weather, but there are some athletes who really push the boundaries of what they can do.

Being the Best

ne of the best-known competitions for snow sports is the Winter Olympic Games. They are held every four years in places all over the world. The first Winter

A snowboard snocross race features tight action and big jumps.

Olympics took place in 1924 in France. The 2018 are set for South Korea. Downhill and cross-country skiing, snowboarding, figure skating, speed skating, and ice hockey are all events at the Winter Olympics. There are also specialized events such as ski jumping and **slalom**, where the skiers or snowboarders zig-zag in between poles. Freestyle skiing and snowboarding, where athletes do aerial tricks, are also part of the Games. One distinctive event at the Winter Olympics is the **biathlon**. It combines skiing and target shooting. The biathlon came out of a tradition in Norway, where soldiers had to learn to do battle on their skis. The International Ski Federation makes the rules for competition in skiing and snowboarding at the Olympics. They also hold their own annual competitions for these events. That way, athletes don't have to wait four years to show off their skills!

Another competition is the Winter X Games, which began in 1997. They are sponsored by the U.S. television sports network ESPN and are held every year. The Winter X Games are known for being extreme—that's what the "X" stands for. Freestyle skiing and snowboarding are the main attractions at these games. Athletes compete in events such as **superpipe** and **slopestyle**. For superpipe, think of a giant straw cut in half the long way, so that it forms a bowl shape. In these events, the walls of the bowl are 22 feet (6.7 m) high, and they go almost straight up. Athletes ski and snowboard up and down the sides of the pipe, performing jumps and tricks as they do. Slopestyle is another challenging event. Athletes go through an obstacle course with jumps and rails, also doing tricks as they go. Speed, precision, and accuracy are important in these events, but so is the athlete's overall performance. They get style points for being original and looking good.

Big Air events are another crowd-pleaser at winter competitions. Skiers and snowboarders climb to a platform some 80 feet (24 m) in the air—that's about eight stories tall! Then they hurtle down a ramp of snow and take off from a jump. Contestants are judged on the difficulty and creativity of the tricks they do in the air before landing. Along

 TRI THIS

In a traditional triathlon, athletes compete in a race that has three separate parts: running, biking, and swimming. A winter triathlon is a little different. Contestants still run and bike, but they do it on hard-packed snow, often on ski trails. Instead of swimming, they do cross-country skiing. A few changes need to be made to adapt a triathlon to the snow. For example, competitors usually ride mountain bikes with wide tires that give them more traction. They may also wear shoes with cleats. For the skiing leg, athletes can use either the "classic" or "skating" style. The skating style is faster, so most contestants choose that.

with difficult spins and flips, sometimes contestants add a little silliness. During a practice run in 2014, an Icelandic snowboarder, Halldor Helgason, took a bite of a banana when he was upside down in the air!

A Big Air snowboarding competition was added to the Olympic lineup for 2018 because these events are so popular with younger contestants and spectators. And big is only getting bigger. For a competition in February 2016, a massive snow ramp was built in Fenway Park, a baseball stadium in Boston, Massachusetts. It was 140 feet (43 m) high!

Pick your Place

Ask skiers or snowboarders where the "best" places to go are, and you will get a lot of different answers. Some people like the Rocky Mountains in Colorado or Wyoming. Others like to go a little farther north, to the Canadian Rockies in British Columbia. The European Alps or the Andes Mountains in South America are also popular destinations. There is no one right answer. Most people go where it is most convenient and they can afford it.

Different areas also offer different types of skiing or snowboarding. It's important to know whether you want deep powder, steep vertical drops, or challenging moguls. Telluride, Colorado; Taos, New Mexico; and Jackson Hole, Wyoming, are places with seriously steep mountainsides, but they are not for beginners! If you've decided to try cross-country skiing or snowshoeing, there are a lot of choices. Those can be done just about anywhere, as long as there's snow.

Finding places to ice skate is a little easier than choosing a ski resort. Most large cities have ice rinks. In colder climates, many smaller towns do too. For the ultimate experience, some skaters like to try out Banff National Park in the Canadian Rockies. It has several indoor and outdoor rinks, and they're all free. Popular places in the United States are Rockefeller Center in New York, or Evergreen Lake, near Denver, Colorado. Evergreen Lake has 8.5 acres of ice, with 11 hockey rinks and a large public skating area.

A skier's dream: A huge field of untouched, unbroken powder.

Snow doesn't have to mean boring days spent inside. A few skills and some basic equipment are great protection against the winter blahs. When the sky turns cloudy, the temperature drops and the snow starts falling, you can start digging your skis out of the garage or your skates out of the closet.

Now . . . where did you put those gloves?

HOW HARD IS IT?

Ski and snowboarding slopes are rated based on how difficult they are. They are marked with symbols to let skiers and boarders know what they're up against. Green circles are the easiest. Blue squares come next. Black diamonds are the most difficult—unless the resort also has a *double* black diamond run. Those are even harder! Skiers or boarders who want special features like jumps or pipes can look for a trail marked with an orange rectangle with rounded corners. There is not an overall standard for rating slopes, however. They are "easy" or "hard" compared to other slopes at the same resort. A green circle run at one place could be harder than a black diamond run at another.

TEXT DEPENDENT QUESTIONS

1. When were the first Winter Olympic Games held?

2. What are the three events in a winter triathlon?

3. Why did the Olympic committee add Big Air snow-boarding to the 2018 lineup?

RESEARCH PROJECT

Check out some of the past results from the Winter Olympic Games or the Winter X Games. What countries have the best athletes in which sports?

FIND OUT MORE

WEBSITES

www.snowlink.com/snow-sports/
Check out this site for how-to tips and videos on skiing, snowboarding, and snowshoeing.

www.olympic.org/sports
The website for the International Olympic Committee has photos, videos, and great information about the history, equipment, and athletes from all sports that are played at the Olympic Games.

BOOKS

Throp, Claire. *Figure Skating*. Oxford, England: Raintree, 2014.

United States Olympic Committee. *A Basic Guide to Skiing and Snowboarding*. New York: Gareth Stevens Publishing, 2002.

Interested in the science of how sports work? Check out the series *Science Behind Sports* from Lucent Books. Titles in the series cover sports including skiing, snowboarding, figure skating, and ice hockey.

bushcraft wilderness skills, named for the remote bush country of Australia

camouflage a pattern or disguise in clothing designed to make it blend into the surroundings

conservation the act of preserving or protecting, such as an environment or species

ecosystem the habitats of species and the ways that species interact with each other

friction the resistance that happens when two surfaces rub together

insulation protection from something, such as extreme hot or cold

layering adding layers of clothing to stay warm and removing layers to cool off.

rewilding returning to a more natural state

synthetic man-made, often to imitate a natural material

traction the grip or contact that an object has with another surface

wake the waves produced by the movement of a boat

INDEX

PHOTO CREDITS

ABOUT THE AUTHOR

Diane Bailey has written about 50 nonfiction books for kids and teens, on topics ranging from science to sports to celebrities. Diane also works as a freelance editor, helping authors who write novels for children and young adults. Diane has two sons and two dogs, and lives in Kansas.